LEAD, FOLLOW OR
GET OUT OF THE WAY

THE ULTIMATE GUIDE TO
LEADERSHIP IN THE
NEW WORLD OF BUSINESS

GREG WITZ
CEO, WITZ EDUCATION

©2014 Greg Witz, Witz Education

Printed in Canada

ISBN-13: 978-1494469832

Witz, Greg, Author

Lead, Follow or Get Out of the Way: The Ultimate Guide to
Leadership in the New World of Business / Greg Witz

ISBN-13: 978-1494469832 (pbk.)

TABLE OF CONTENTS

PREFACE

This book is about leadership. Why? Because we are all leaders. And we are all followers. There are those who have influenced us on our path in life and there are those who we influence and guide. And those teachers, the ones who impact us the most, are often the people we least expect. The ones who, with a small gesture or a few words of wisdom steered us in the right direction. This book is for the inspirers, the impacters, the challengers and the motivators. Those who strive to be better for their teams, for their families and for themselves.

Through my years in business I have worked my way up the ladder. I have been the guy in the mailroom trying to catch a break, been the sales manager trying to push and encourage my team, been the VP working under a very powerful and influential man, my father, and have now become President and CEO of my own company, Witz Education. I have developed courses and keynotes, coached individuals, managers and CEOs, and taught thousands of people how to deal with people.

Because at the core of it, leadership is just that - how to deal with people. Not deal with them in the "forced to handle them" sense, but deal with them in the "inspire greatness in them" sense. And that is what I do. I inspire my team everyday to perform and then outperform. And more importantly, I inspire fellow CEOs, managers and leaders to inspire others.

I am just a guy. A guy who found the balance. A guy who sits in his office every day, watching greatness develop around me. Watching, encouraging, inspiring...leading. This book is everything I know...well all the important stuff anyway. It is a step-by-step guide into understanding those you "deal" with on a daily basis. That could be your office team, your kids, your spouse, your overly involved mother-in-law, or the customer service person on the phone.

Let's face it, the world has changed in a big way. And business has changed. Gone are the days of corporate ladders, yearly performance reviews, a hard day's work is a hard day's pay. Welcome to the world of smart phones and social media, of young geniuses and working from home. Baby Boomers are on the way out and Gen X and Y are roaring in to take over the 15-million-job void that will be left behind. And this younger generation is coming full force to lead our companies, our governments and our world. It's a very new game and it's time to get in it or risk freezing into the dark ages on the sidelines.

But have no fear. This is an exciting time. Reading this book will provide you and your business with the competitive edge you need to become the trendsetters in your industry, to blow your competitors out of the water and to positively impact your bottom line. The secret doesn't lie in higher efficiencies, or new product innovations or better sales people. It lies in leadership.

So here it is... the no BS approach to leadership. The no-nonsense, give it to you straight reality of leading and succeeding in the new business world. Whether you are a Boomer CEO who is trying to balance multiple generations in your company, an emerging entrepreneur striving to be taken seriously or a busy mom raising 3 kids, these next pages will inspire you to own your role as a leader and succeed by helping those around you win. And by win, I do mean grow your business, make more money, impact your industry and take all your cheerleaders along for the ride.

Remember that as you read this book.

CHAPTER ONE

WHAT IT ALL MEANS FOR LEADERS

Since the beginning of time it has been in our human nature to categorize ourselves and others. Whether it be by gender, race, age or religion, we have an inherent need to identify with others by defining them and therefore defining ourselves.

Identifying as part of a "generation" has really only been occurring since the late 18th century. One of the first distinguished generations was the "Family Generation". This was defined either as time it took for a mother to raise her children from the birth of the first born or by the time between a mother having her first child and her daughter having her first child. This later became defined as the average age of a woman having her first child (25 years old).

As the 19th century continued and modernism, industrialism and westernization all began to contribute to our definition of self, the idea formed into social generations. It morphed into a way to categorize or define peoples' behaviour, acts, ideas and opinions.

In the 1950's, the workplace was comprised of people whose value systems and work ethics were strongly influenced by the Great Depression and two World Wars. This Silent Generation as they are known, born between 1925 and 1945, expressed strong appreciation for the opportunity to have a job and were typically very loyal to the company they worked for. There was an inherent belief that the boss was always right. Management style was patriarchal: management was the brains and the labor was the brawn.

This attitude began to change with the spawning of a more service-based economy. Enter the Baby Boomers. Those individuals born between 1946 and 1964. This group rejected the old ways of blindly following the path laid out by their employers. They wanted more influence on how the workplace was run; they wanted participatory management. Baby Boomers saw their job as a source of personal identity and didn't readily embrace the Silent Generation's view that workers should be seen and not heard. Boomers were willing to work hard and sacrifice to achieve the American dream of having it all.

Then along came Generation X whose attitudes about the workplace were shaped by observing their frantic parents running through the economic rat race. They watched as their parents became victims of corporate mergers and lay-offs. As they observed the effects this had, many Gen Xers, born between 1965 and 1980, abandoned the workaholic attitude of the Boomers and decided to do things differently. They would not be consumed by the demands of the workplace. They would certainly not be slackers either, just not as invested in being a personal extension of their job.

Generation X also shook up management styles in the workplace. Traditional methods of top down management did not have the same impact on this generation. They grew by questioning authority and challenging old ways of thinking. This generation wanted the authority to participate in the day-to-day decision-making and long-term planning of the company that employed them.

And now Generations Y and Z have entered the workforce feeling entitled and instantaneous, and with good reason. These generations, Y born between 1981 and 1995, and Z born between 1996 and 2012 are by far the most educated in terms of book smarts. They are also the most connected in terms of technology and social media. Gen Z's bring entrepreneurialism to an extreme. Much like Gen Y's they would prefer to work in a medium sized business and are less influenced by money. Having seen the recession's impact on their parents and older siblings, meaningful work takes precedence over money.

Gen Z's want to be taken seriously and believe the workplace should be more about ideas and contributions than age rank. They want to get their feet wet and be involved right away, not wait years to have that chance. They want to work for an honest and transparent leader that can coach and mentor them. They are eager to learn and to establish themselves in their roles. They bring innovation, new thinking and big ideas. And whether we like it or not, they will be the next generations to fill the job gap left by retiring Boomers.

We now have four distinct generations working alongside each other to form today's workplace. They operate differently. They think differently. They listen differently. They are engaged differently. They want different things from their jobs and from their leaders. So what, as leaders, are we to do? How do we evolve our leadership styles to include the structured, task-oriented, no news is good news, I learned the hard way so you can too Baby Boomer, alongside the do more in less time, work flexible hours, let's meet and collaborate Gen Y?

Perhaps you are a Boomer trying to find the balance within your organization. Maybe you are an entrepreneurial Gen X who employs Boomers and Gen Ys. Or perhaps you are a Gen Y looking for ways to assert yourself and demand respect in the workplace. It is a leadership transition the likes of which corporate America has never seen before. The stark differences in values between generations have never been so real.

All the answers lie in leadership.

CHAPTER TWO

THE LEADERSHIP STYLES

What type of leader are you? Have you ever sat down and considered what your leadership style is and how it's working, or isn't working? How do you think the people you lead would describe your style? Authoritative? Nurturing? Spontaneous? Rational?

Every person, regardless of their position in a company, regardless of their role or their generation, has a style of communication that we call their default ego state. This is the style of communicating that a person has learned and adopted over the course of their life and experiences. For leaders, the style in which they habitually interact and communicate with others becomes their preferred leadership state. The challenge is for leaders to understand their default style and recognize where they need to modify it in order to communicate effectively.

According to transactional analysis, a theory of modern psychology based on the work of Dr. Eric Berne, when two people interact, a transaction occurs. I say or do something to you and you respond. Berne believed that every person is made up of three ego states: Parent, Child, and Adult. The Parent ego state represents the voice of authority and is formed by external events and influences over the course of our childhood. The Parent ego embodies phrases such as "always", "never forget" "don't do that", and "do it this way".

The Child ego state in contrast, is based on our internal reactions and feelings to external events. According to Berne, this is the hearing, feeling and emotional body of data within each of us. When anger or despair dominates reason, then our inner child is in control (Berne, 1957).

Our Adult ego state is our ability to think and rationally determine actions for ourselves based on data received. Instead of finger pointing or posturing body language that shows up in the Parent ego state or squirming temper tantrum type behavior exhibited by the Child state, the Adult ego position is non-threatening and non-threatened. The Adult state is confident, mature and rational above all else. When two people both interact from their Adult ego state, communication is most effective.

We have identified six distinct ego states or styles, each with its own positive and negative qualities. All six ego states have a typical pattern of behaviour. We each use all of these ego states in our daily lives, both personally and professionally. We may have certain ego states that are more comfortable for us and become our default ego states. No one ego state is good or bad. It is more a matter of identifying which ego state will serve you best in each communication and learning how to dial one ego state up or down to get the result you want. Understanding who you are and who the person you are talking to is, will help you to guide every interaction into effective communication. In order to be a successful leader, you not only have to understand your preferred ego state but be constantly modifying it to apply to your staff and particular situation.

1. Critical Parent Leadership
2. Nurturing Parent Leadership
3. Spontaneous Child Leadership
4. Withdrawn Child Leadership
5. Angry Child Leadership
6. Adult Leadership

CRITICAL PARENT LEADERSHIP

 When acting and communicating from the Critical Parent style, leaders are direct, clear and assertive. Often demanding, this style drives performance, pushes limits and relies heavily on rules, standards and processes. The CP leader is authoritative and commands obedience from their position as Boss. Boomers will particularly resonate with CP leaders as this is the style they notoriously grew up modeling.

When Critical Parent is excessive, it takes on a more rigid and overbearing style that tends to stifle creativity and creates a fearful environment. In response to excessive CP Leadership, people will tend to play it safe or revert to their own Child ego position. When this happens, communication breaks down and effectiveness is lost.

When the Critical Parent ego state is not dialed up enough, leaders may not be taken seriously as the authority in their organization. Timelines may not be met, projects remain incomplete and employees may not take on tasks or responsibilities with a sense of priority.

Leaders become immobile and incapable of decision making, voicing opinions or taking action.

Finding the balance between excessive and insufficient is critical for those with the default Critical Parent ego state. At their best CP leaders are balanced and assertive without being confrontational. They are open to views other than their own. They know how to engage a team and they can command enough authority to ensure employee responsibility and accountability. They create an environment of respect and enthusiasm.

NURTURING PARENT LEADERSHIP

The Nurturing Parent ego state represents exactly what you may be thinking. Picture a kind, protective mother baking cookies and giving everyone hugs and kisses. Nurturing Parents are patient, accepting and sensitive.

The Nurturing Parent style of leadership shows up in organizations where significant value is placed on mentoring and coaching. This occurs when an individual's potential

17

is recognized and they are given opportunities to learn and receive constant feedback. In contrast to the Critical Parent leadership style, where privilege is earned in the long term, Nurturing Parent leaders believe that positive reinforcement, acknowledgement and rewards are more effective. NP leadership style is attractive and required by today's Generations Y and Z, as it appeals to their need for inclusion.

If the Nurturing Parent style reverts to extremes, it will show up in behavior that is smothering, vague and overly accommodating. Excessive NP leaders inadvertently enable bad behavior (missed deadlines, not being taken seriously) and get taken advantage of. If allowed to dominate, Excessive Nurturing Parent leaders eventually lose the respect and authority they have worked hard to attain.

Insufficient NP leaders often appear aloof and uncomfortable offering compliments or feedback. There are no public displays of affection from these guys (and gals)!

Nurturing Parent Leaders at their best are attentive, empathetic and encourage ongoing dialogue with their teams. Nancy, a client of mine and a mid level manager at a large printing company, embodied the perfect balance of Nurturing Parent in her role. She took the time to get to know each member of her team. She built rapport and trust with everyone. She encouraged her team to find new solutions or ways of doing things. This actually resulted in some policy changes across the company. Because Nancy took the time to coach and mentor the team members she worked with, they were engaged, her employee retention was high and they outperformed other teams within the company. The Nurturing Parent ego state can be extremely effective especially among younger generations to help motivate and encourage peak performance.

SPONTANEOUS CHILD LEADERSHIP

 The Spontaneous Child leader sounds like fun, and indeed they can be. They are enthusiastic, optimistic and full of energy. The SC leader motivates, inspires and creates a culture of creative thinking and possibilities. Staff get caught up in the momentum, and performance levels and morale are bolstered. Spontaneous Child leaders love the excitement of technology and look for opportunities to operate outside of their local geography. This style is also attractive to Gens Y and Z and the more entrepreneurial Xers. Easily distracted, sarcastic and cavalier, they jump to conclusions and suffer credibility issues over the long term. Because the SC is often quick to react, rash decisions and judgements can sometimes jeopardize the direction of a company and the trust of its team members.

Without a healthy dose of Spontaneous Child however, leaders with a deficiency of SC tend to be rather boring, fearful and take the world and themselves way too seriously. They appear reserved, stressed out and rigid. Leaders with an insufficient Spontaneous Child ego state can seem anti-social and disengaged.

At their best, SC leaders embrace curiosity, creativity and differing perspectives. They embody a sense of lightheartedness. They are friendly and sociable. A good time to use your Spontaneous Child ego state as a leader is when trying to inspire people or to get them to buy into an idea. SC leaders can look at things from a different angle, think outside the box and tend not to sweat the small stuff.

WITHDRAWN CHILD LEADERSHIP

At first, the idea of Withdrawn Child can seem negative, but there is a lot of value in this style of leadership. A Withdrawn Child leader tends to be cautious, methodical and reflective. Supremely attentive to process and procedure, WC shows up in positive attributes such as a strong ability to plan, adapt and consider all the alternatives before jumping into a project. They want to follow systems that are proven and value discretion and common sense, traits most Boomers grew up modeling. WC leaders prefer working independently, and are

20

adverse to accepting ownership of projects, but prefer to take responsibility over collaboration.

In excess, Withdrawn Child leaders appear apathetic, too risk adverse and more interested in technological interactions than human connections. They might choose to send an email to an employee about a problem in order to avoid a face to face interaction. They appear introverted, shy and private. As a leader, an excessive Withdrawn Child ego state can show up to staff as disinterest or an unwillingness to take things on. Excessive WC leaders fester and hold on to things. At their worst, WC leaders are emotionally unavailable and unable to work collaboratively in teams. They can and often do conceal feelings of frustration, anger and resentment, causing teams and projects to implode.

An appropriate level of the Withdrawn Child ego state in a leader can help with reflecting on decisions, considering all perspectives and not jumping into things. A good time to use your WC ego state is when discretion is required. The WC leader understands timing and communication in sensitive situations.

ANGRY CHILD LEADERSHIP

Similar to the Critical Parent style of leadership, Angry Child leaders are driven, demanding and competitive. They are relentless in goal achievement and have a never quit attitude. The Angry Child is positive in that they are self motivating and naturally able to challenge themselves and their team members, which encourages innovation and pushes through barriers. Many well known Gen Xers would fall into this category of leadership style.

In excess though, Angry Child leaders resemble children who have stayed up well past their bedtime. Impatient, volatile and reactive, excessive AC leaders can cause serious damage to relationships and productivity. Communication breaks down at all levels and trust is eroded. They can be aggressive and let frustrations get the better of them. If leaders find themselves too accepting of delays and excuses, it fosters a passive and even more volatile reaction when faced with stress.

An appropriate time to use the Angry Child ego state is when trying to push team members out of their comfort zone. The AC leader is not afraid to take a risk or make a decision. Coming from the Angry Child ego state can be a great motivator to change.

ADULT LEADERSHIP

Adult Leadership represents a mature and rational style that is calculating and open. They are long term big picture thinkers and understand how and when to delegate and empower their team members. Adult Leaders logically evaluate situations and make wise decisions that benefit themselves, their team and their organizations. At their best, leaders with the Adult style as their preferred ego state are calm, adaptable and reliable.

In excess, the Adult Leadership ego state can get caught up in the details, over-analyzing to the point of inaction. Think of Mr. Spock from the famous Star Trek series. The Excessive Adult Leader appears indifferent to the human side of business but if Adult Leader is insufficient, they can procrastinate making decisions to the point that opportunities are lost. The Adult leadership state can be black and white thinking at its best and worst.

When in doubt, approaching any situation from the Adult ego state will net good results. The Adult ego state is investigative, asking questions to better understand circumstances. When leaders use the Adult ego state in interactions, it often pushes those with whom they are interacting into the Adult ego state as well. This helps to take emotions out of the picture and brings things to a rational point of view.

To be clear, each leadership style has its strengths and weaknesses, there is no one size fits all solution. In an ideal situation the leadership style will be adapted to elicit the desired response from the person you are communicating with. The more both parties in the transaction approach the conversation from their Adult ego state, the more productive and successful the outcome. This isn't as easy as it may sound. Most of us have particular situations and people that act as triggers to our preferred style of communication. Understanding what those triggers are and managing them effectively is the key for leaders of the future.

Boomers may be comfortable with the Critical Parent style of leadership, keeping their head down and getting the job done. But Generations Y and Z simply won't stick around. Their inherent confidence and level of self respect has taught them that they deserve to be treated as a peer. They want feedback and the opportunity to collaborate which means that you might need to adopt a more Nurturing Parent style of communication in order to keep them engaged.

Every team has varying needs, abilities and generations at play, and the most successful leaders will be those who can capitalize on the styles available. Beginning first with themselves.

CHAPTER THREE

LEAD YOURSELF FIRST

Leaders do not command excellence, they build it.

To reach excellence, you must first be a leader of good character. Do everything you are "supposed" to do. Leaders will not achieve excellence by first deciding where they want to go, then doing whatever it takes to get there, then hoping to act as a leader with good character. Pursuing excellence should not be confused with accomplishing a job or task. Excellence begins with leaders of good and strong character who engage in the entire process of leadership.

Character develops over time. It does not change quickly. A person with strong character shows drive, energy, determination, self-discipline, willpower and nerve. A leader's actions set the pace for the organization. A strong vision for the future aligns the team. Strong character in a leader builds trust and loyalty. So how do you get there as a leader? How do you build excellence within your organization and more importantly, within yourself? Let's begin by looking at the qualities of great leadership.

I've worked with and coached hundreds of high performance leaders. Everyone from the budding Gen X entrepreneur to CEOs of Fortune 500 companies to the Canadian and US governments. Over the years I have compiled a list of the top ten qualities they possess. Qualities that set them apart, that make them great and inspire greatness in their teams. And you can bet that leaders who are at the top of their game are well disciplined at these characteristics.

Do you have what it takes or the desire to have what it takes to be a high performance leader? As you read through this list, take some time to think about how well you are doing in each area. Think about employee retention rates in your organization, the cost of hiring someone new, the multiple generations within your team, the culture within your company, the motivation of your staff.

This is my challenge to you. Don't just read this list. If you are a leader, a true leader, a leader who wants to make a positive dent on a little part of the universe, who wants to inspire and create and build and succeed, you must see this as a challenge. A never-ending daily challenge to strive for excellence. You will know when you get there – to that point of pure excellence as a leader - because it will be the day you retire, likely at a very old age, not because you had to work all those years but because you loved your work and your team and the greatness you developed in others and yourself.

1. Progress, Not Failure
2. Optimism & the Ability to Inspire
3. Compassion
4. Humility
5. Servant Leadership
6. Creative Thinking
7. Tenacity
8. Transparency
9. Risk Taking
10. World Perspective

CHAPTER FOUR

PROGRESS, NOT FAILURE

Everyone makes mistakes, but leaders are more likely to fail with larger audiences. What makes a person an exceptional leader though, is their ability to acknowledge and learn from their mistakes; big or small.

We've all worked with or for a boss who charged through the office like a tornado. My way or the highway oozes from their every pore. And depending on where you sat in the chain of command, they either made your life miserable or you simply just kept your head down and did your job, all the while secretly job hunting. When you finally did resign or were fired during one of the boss' irrational explosions, you can rest assured that the boss placed all the failure on your shoulders. "He was an idiot, he was lazy, she was incompetent anyway, etc," is how this type of boss would rationalize it. Rarely would a leader like that reflect on how their leadership style and company culture could be the causes. Instead they would blame their high turnover rate and costs of talent acquisition on "the lazy generation Ys " they are being forced to hire.

A boss like this would even read the recent Gallup poll (2011) of over a million corporate workers that identified bad bosses, and not salary issues, as the number one reason people quit as fluff and excuses for low performance. Thankfully though, bosses like that don't get very far in the long term, regardless of the generational context, and they definitely won't succeed moving into the future. The future demands a different kind of leader, one who recognizes their influence on situations and people at every turn.

Great leaders, the kind I know you aspire to be (because you're reading this book), look at situations and people through a different lens and that lens is self awareness. If people are quitting around you, you're not reaching the success you want or you find yourself complaining about the same scenario that shows up day after day at work and even at home, I guarantee you – it's not them – it's YOU. There is something in your style of communication that isn't working. And it's up to you and only you to change it. You need to understand your preferred ego state and learn how to adapt and modify it to the people and situations under your influence.

At some point, the CEO or Manager hits a proverbial rock bottom and realizes that something needs to change. But they don't know exactly what, and they definitely don't know how. This is the story of Mark.

I met Mark at a leadership seminar I was conducting, when he approached me after the session. He told me that a key member of his management team had recently resigned and the rest of his team was taking the loss exceptionally hard. He could tell that they blamed him, not only for the quitting of their top sales person, but the exodus of quite a few great staff members over the last few years. After an especially candid staff meeting, it was made very clear to Mark that these employees hadn't quit because of the workload or for more money, but had jumped ship because of Mark, and the rest of the team was ready to walk too. Mark felt like a huge failure and wasn't sure what to do. I smiled at him and was met with a look of confusion. "This is great Mark, and here's why," I said, "This experience, this aha moment of realization and self awareness is what is going to help you change from being a Bully Boss to a Great Leader." "Really?" he replied, "How?"

The first step of our leadership program is for participants to take our Multi-Rater Personality Inventory. The MRPI is a behavioral measurement tool based on Dr. Eric Berne's theory of structural analysis; the analysis of an individual's personality. At my company, we took this structural analysis a step further by creating a measurement tool that measures tangible attributes concerning communication styles, leadership, management, stress responses, assertiveness and emotional reactions. The MRPI helps leaders and managers learn about themselves and the people they lead, so they can optimize behavioral and personal competencies to accelerate performance.

We then also consider the generational influences at play. Mark was a Boomer, that is he was born between 1946 and 1964, but the majority of his staff are Gen X and Y. So while Mark had grown up modeling the Critical Parent style of management, it clearly wasn't effective any longer. As we talked about how Mark's style showed up in all sorts of situations both at work and in his personal life, it was clear that Mark was going to need to adapt his communication style to the people he was leading.

Our coaching sessions weren't "Let's beat up Mark!" On the contrary, and this is why embracing failure is so important, it's about learning how to adapt Mark's style of leadership into what his team needs to perform at optimal levels, versus what Mark's preferred or default style is. As we went through a few of Mark's "failures" and had his team take the MRPI Assessment, we easily identified ways that Mark could shift his approach and change the outcome.

Great leaders do this **ALL THE TIME**, and that's why they get better and better at everything. They spend a portion of their day reflecting on their own actions and approaches and how they impacted the results they got. By working collectively with the entire team, everyone learns about themselves and those around them. Conversations are more productive, morale and engagement are increased and the bottom line grows. Great leaders attract deeper relationships that produce bigger results. The people they lead are no longer just employees but engaged members of the **TEAM** – all working towards a common goal.

Great leaders don't wallow in the mistakes they make, heck, who has time for that? By viewing failure of any kind as opportunities for growth and expansion, at the business and personal level you will become a more gifted leader. Great leaders make adjustments in their approach and remain optimistic about their own personal development.

CHAPTER FIVE

OPTIMISM & THE ABILITY TO INSPIRE

I define optimism as hopefulness mixed with confidence. It is a quality that all great leaders share. The ability to see the good, the successes, and the progress in everything they do, and especially in the people they lead. Great leaders focus on what's positive and build on it, creating confidence and optimism in those around them.

That isn't to say that great leaders are "Polly Anna's" or anything of the sort, but they embrace their setbacks, learn from them and keep going. We've all experienced dark and bad times. New competitors, dismal economic outlooks and even downright business failures. In spite of these setbacks, great leaders keep a cool and confident head.

While optimism shows up at work differently based on generational perspectives, it is a characteristic that all great leaders have in common. Great leaders are self aware enough to know their own style of optimism and how to utilize it to affect and influence those they lead. When a CEO or manager is optimistic they are usually gifted in their ability to use that, not only to self motivate, but to motivate and inspire others.

"If you treat an individual as he is, he will stay as he is, but if you treat him as if he were what he ought and could be, he will become what he ought and could be" Johann Wolfgang Von Goethe (1749-1832)

Success at something, regardless of how big or small, breeds confidence and optimism, which then leads to more success and the circle continues. Knowing how to get the wheel started is what great leaders do. Great leaders don't subscribe to the status quo. They use their gift of optimism to create a culture of growth, advancement and striving. They embrace the Spontaneous Child ego state. Self awareness plays a critical function in this area because as leaders, knowing how their approach influences others, is the impetus of motivating positive action or de-motivating to the point of inertia. We've all been around bosses and managers who bring out or trigger our best qualities and those who trigger our faults, anger, resentment or depression. When a leader understands his or her team members enough, they will naturally focus on what a specific team member needs in a situation.

Take for example, you work for an Angry Child style of leader and you make a mistake. At their best, Angry Child leaders push through barriers and are highly competitive and self motivating – they get things done. Perhaps you lost a sale or a potential new customer. If the leader isn't aware of their Angry Child style of leadership, they will typically revert into extreme modes of behavior by becoming reactive, volatile and extremely impatient.

Depending on your own internal systems, you're likely to take the assault on your character very personally, responding in anger or reverting to withdrawn depression. Self talk is negative and your optimism is extinguished. But, if the leader is aware of their default leadership style, the situation can be managed differently, focusing on problem solving without personal attacks. This makes the entire exercise a learning opportunity and builds trust between the leader and their team.

How do you become more optimistic and confident if it doesn't come naturally to you? If you haven't gleaned it yet, the secret is in self awareness and ultimately being excited by life; your Spontaneous Child! If you aren't excited about the journey, you are on the wrong path! How will you be able to excite others around you? Now this doesn't mean you need to shake your pom-poms and do cartwheels around the office, but it does mean that you walk with a spring in your step and a vibe of passion, urgency, desire, energy and animation that others just can't help but be compelled by.

Wake yourself up with a mantra and repeat it to yourself all day every day, until it is engrained in you. Life is good and it is short. I promise you, being positive will affect every aspect of your life. So work on changing your perspective. I'm not saying you should be naive or unrealistic. You should never operate under false pretenses. But you should strive to look at the glass half full, to crack a joke in a tense moment and to smile at everyone around you.

Leadership does not simply reside in the office. It embodies you and your character. Therefore, doing things outside of the office to get you excited about life will resonate with your organization. Whether it's yoga or sky diving, reading a book or public speaking, doing a good deed for a stranger or teaching your kid to ride a bike, do things everyday to keep yourself motivated and in turn motivating others.

CHAPTER SIX

COMPASSION -
BEING AUTHENTIC
AT WORK

I hope you're picking up on the pattern I'm laying out. Great leadership is nothing more than the ability to relate and communicate with others. The more you can grasp that and remove ego from your relationships and situations, the stronger you'll become as a great leader.

We've all heard the saying "people don't care how much you know until they know how much you care" and leaders, those who aspire to be great, understand this more than anything. It doesn't matter how many degrees you have or how many credentials you list after your name on a business card, great leaders are great because they share the qualities of compassion and empathy in their relationships. To succeed as a leader in the future, compassion may very well dictate how far you go – and frankly, you Boomers reading this – you more than any other generation will likely have the hardest time adapting and accepting this new reality. But the future demands you adapt or die.

The first step involves a great degree of self-awareness, self-esteem and compassion, getting in touch with your Nurturing Parent ego state. The best leaders, great leaders, are excellent at watching how others react to them and fine-tuning their communication style to ensure they are building the relationship. This doesn't mean that they change their mind at every turn to get people to like them, or that they waver on their goals. Rather, it's about finding alternate ways of saying things so that their team is motivated, encouraged, dedicated and clear. By taking steps towards the Nurturing Parent style of leadership, and understanding what position their team members are in, compassionate leaders breed success in their teams and their organizations.

Masters at leadership know that power resides in the relationship and that all relationships begin and end with how you perceive yourself and how others perceive you. Now, you may not think that how you feel about yourself has a whole lot to do with how others perceive you, but you are wrong. In my experiences as a coach and trainer, low self esteem is directly correlated with stagnant companies and struggling leaders. Every individual is their own best friend and their own worst enemy.

Sure, dealing with self esteem can seem like a touchy-feely waste of time but it is crucial to your success as a leader. More often than not, the leaders I coach are looking for guidance in working through a situation where their level of belief in themselves is hindering them. For great leaders, because they have the high level of optimism we talked about, moments of low self esteem are mostly situational, but they indeed come up for everyone. Recognizing that we all have moments where we doubt ourselves and being compassionate first with ourselves, will cultivate a deeper level of compassion for and understanding of with those you lead. Without compassion, real compassion for the human beings who make up your team, you aren't likely to develop trust, and without it it's impossible to create healthy and productive environments.

Be assured that as the leader, you are being watched all the time and your values and integrity are being assessed. People need to be assured that their trust, followed closely by their respect, is in a safe place and that they are wise to follow where you lead. When people trust you, they are more willing to give their best and feel confident that they will get your best. Your team will shift into more Adult leadership behavior instead of Withdrawn Child responses. Trust is built by showing compassion to those you lead. As they open up and share more about themselves, their goals and desires, and if you are compassionate in listening and really try to sit on their side of the table, you'll earn their trust and respect – not because you're the boss – but because you care.

CHAPTER SEVEN

HUMILITY-
IT ISN'T THE HOW,
IT'S THE WHAT

Humility, the ability to keep your feet on the ground and your ego in check even if you really are the smartest one at the table, is another of the somewhat fluffier qualities that books on leadership rarely discuss. But don't mistake that for lack of importance. Great leaders are highly skilled at remaining humble and showing humility. Unlike their predecessors, Gen Ys and Zs are not attracted to leaders who exhibit behaviors of overconfident arrogance or authority. Nope, these young, connected and extremely bright individuals will demand that they and those around them are recognized as equals and unique. This change from the old school leadership styles will be drastic and if you're not prepared for it – catastrophic.

Please don't take this as a rally cry for lack of pride in your accomplishments. Being proud of yourself, your team and your company, isn't a flaw. What I am talking about is putting your attention on how you behave and interact with others, during good times and bad. Gone are the days of closed door executive offices. You must have noticed that your team wants and needs access to you. Being arrogant or self important instead of employing a bit of modesty would effectively slam that door in their faces, incinerating any depth of trust or relationship.

Great leaders know how to enjoy and share their successes without letting it "go to their heads". Remember Mark from Chapter Four? At the heart of the issue was the need for Mark to come down off his pedestal and gain a clearer perspective of himself in the context of his team. He had to embrace a little Withdrawn Child, be reflective and then allow the Nurturing Parent leadership style to take stage. Mark had to recognize that he wouldn't have achieved the success he enjoyed without the support of his team, those hard working individuals who looked after clients and effectively ran the office so he could do what he does best. Humbling himself to the reality of his circumstances and letting his team see his genuine humility has been life changing, not only professionally but personally too.

Humility shows up differently in the eyes of those you lead. Who doesn't love a hero or a success story? But what we don't like, in fact we find it extremely unbecoming, is arrogance. As the Xers move upward and the Ys and Zs take foothold from the Boomers at work, respect and trust will be harder for leaders to earn. Especially for those who run around patting themselves on the back, announcing their superiority and flaunting their success to everyone around them. The future will have no time for Bully and Diva behaviors regardless of their position. With entrepreneurship becoming the model of business in the future and globalization opening up borders and perspectives, people and clients will look to work for and do business with people who have both feet firmly planted.

CHAPTER EIGHT

SERVANT LEADERSHIP

In the future, growing a company will require more attention on your people than anything else.

Younger generations are demanding personal growth from their jobs. The responsibility of a great leader is to establish an environment where people can be mentored, where they have freedom and encouragement to continuously learn. That is what servant leadership is about. No longer is it just you who should be the superstar. You must build a team of stars around you and a servant leader puts the emphasis on the needs of the team over their own.

A great leader fosters a culture of achievement and growth by including their team in decision making, keeping the organization as flat as possible and challenging their team with new responsibilities that encourage personal growth. They create systems and structures that ensure that every member of the organization is pushing the envelope. In my experience teaching and coaching multiple generations, here are the key areas where great leaders focus to create a culture of servant leadership.

MENTORING

Generations X, Y and Z require and want coaching. They want to learn from their leaders. They want to understand the entire operation of the company they are working for and how their specific roles impact that. Millennials don't want specific roles in the sense that they are boxed into a job. They want the freedom to be involved on projects, to be accountable and to work with teams. These generations prefer an open door policy where they can seek feedback or leadership at any time.

Not surprisingly, the younger generations are not keen to sit behind their desks staring at a computer all day. They want dialogue, communication and social interaction. Although they are self-starters, they thrive in a collaborative environment. They want to be able to knock on their leader's door anytime to share a thought or ask a question. They want new challenges to constantly keep their jobs interesting and dynamic. They demand a leader who can balance their Adult ego state with a Nurturing Parent style of leadership.

VALUE THEIR VALUES

Gen Xers are family oriented and place a high value on work-life balance. Gen Ys believe even more strongly that a job doesn't define them and that four walls of an office do not confine them to their job. While Boomers might believe in working late, getting in early and that the more hours they put in at the office the more loyal and productive they are, the younger generations feel they can contribute to their jobs without physically being in the office and prefer the flexibility to make their own schedules.

There is something we can all learn from this style of work. Gen X and Y are in no way less effective or produce lower results. They manage to get it all done and still be home for dinner. Why? Well, they leverage technology to speed up the process, the internet to help with research and social media to share ideas. And because they are always connected, many of them have answered emails on the subway ride into work, or finished that report at 10pm after the kids have gone to bed.

Accommodating their requests for flexible "time in the office" will help your organization. If you find you are getting pushback from your Boomer employees, consider equipping them with the tools to be more mobile as well. You will breed loyalty and work ethic into your younger employees. And we all know loyalty leads to less turnover and impacts your bottom line.

ASK QUESTIONS

Giving your employees, young or old, what they feel they need to be most successful in their jobs, will encourage respect and trust. Don't be afraid to ask each of your employees how you can help them. Remember, you don't always have to say yes to every request. But you will never know unless you ask.

Perhaps the reason Sally from accounting has become so withdrawn and resentful is because she hates having to drive for two hours each day in rush hour traffic to get home and she hasn't been able to put her kids to bed in months. All she wants is to be able to leave at 4:30 instead of 5:00. Easy fix.

John in sales has been slipping lately because his GPS is broken and he is finding it challenging to find his way to meetings. Simple – new GPS equals new, happy John. New, happy John equals better sales results which equals better profits.

FOCUS ON RETENTION

Employee retention has certainly become much more challenging. With so much competition, employees feel a greater sense of freedom to choose a job based on their needs. Meeting those needs, especially when that employee is a great employee and a huge asset to your company, is essential. We all know the worst thing is to spend a year teaching a new employee the ropes and bringing them to their full potential in their role, only to have them leave you.

So what are some of the challenges with retaining employees today? Older workers leave believing that "these young kids" climbing the company ladder have no idea how to lead. Younger generations leave feeling that no one at the company is taking them seriously. How do we empower them both? Try pairing them up. Remember, the Boomers have the knowledge and experience and the Gen Xs and Ys are eager to learn. Create a partnership program where both parties have the opportunity to teach something to the other.

CULTURE IS EVERYTHING

Culture is key but it is also absolutely the hardest thing to build into a company. And it starts from the top. No matter what your company does, I would assert you want your entire team to say "I love working there", "I feel so supported", and "I have the best team". Culture does not lie in company pot lucks and holiday parties. It doesn't lie in Friday afternoons off in the summer or bring your kid to work days. It lies in the leader who serves.

CHAPTER NINE

CREATIVE THINKING -
THE RISE OF
THE RIGHT BRAIN

It's no longer sufficient to "think outside the box" as the maxim goes. Leadership in the future requires innovative thinking, gleaning inspiration from multiple sources and perspectives and embracing the creative thinking of your entire team.

But I'm not creative, you say!

I hear you. But that's a lie. The truth is that we are all creative in some way but instead of encouraging it, the work world has tended to dismiss it. If you weren't running an advertising agency or design firm, creativity was frowned upon. Thankfully, the world has changed and we are seeing what Daniel Pink meant in his book *A Whole New Mind (2006)*... The rise of the Right Brain. Hooray for all the closet poets out there!

Creative thinking is now being recognized for directly and positively impacting a company's bottom line. It's the responsibility of those individuals in leadership positions to encourage their team to draw outside the lines, to bring forward any ideas and foster curiosity amongst their team. Seems to me that our natural instinct of curiosity has been stifled for far too long, with leaders and corporations of all sizes resting on the "this is how it's done in our industry." This mode of thinking won't survive in the future and if leaders don't embrace creativity and their inner Spontaneous Child, their companies are sure to suffer. For those that do embrace creative thinking and a commitment to innovation, they'll be rewarded significantly. Choose wisely but know that even small steps towards being more creative will net you results.

One of my friends, a management consultant, recently shared the following story with me and I think it illustrates beautifully what can be accomplished by taking off the blinders. My friend had been approached by a medium sized manufacturing firm to develop a five year strategic plan. It was clear from the first discovery session with the leadership team that not much had changed in the company's operations over their thirty year history. The company wasn't utilizing available technologies that would allow them more access to current and prospective customers, and they were firmly entrenched in only looking within their industry for information and opportunities. Growth was slow and it was taking more effort than ever to land new business. Having experience working with the banking, pharmaceutical and professional services industries, she shared with this manufacturing company some examples of how these different industries have been evolving their marketing and customer service departments. Her client was not only fascinated but open to implementing a few of the ideas shared.

This was a big step for the company but almost immediately they started to see the positive impact. Something as simple as reorganizing their current clients into niche categories and assigning them a dedicated account manager, was netting huge results. In the 16th Annual Global CEO Survey (2013) conducted by Price Waterhouse Coopers, it highlighted that 82% of CEO's plan to change their customer strategies and my friend's client was no different. With more and more competition from local and overseas competitors, it was imperative that this manufacturer get closer to their customers and foster deeper, more loyal relationships. Shifting the trend from having their products seen as commodities purchased only on price to becoming a strategic partner who understands and helps drive profitability for all, was the goal.

By dedicating an account manager to client files instead of having whoever happened to answer the 1-800 number taking orders, the sales team has noticed a huge change in their department. Not only are sales figures up, clients who in the past had no real concept of the full array of services this manufacturer offered, began inviting the company to the table during planning and engineering sessions. On top of that, this shift in approach gave the account team a real sense of responsibility and focus, which has increased morale and teamwork!

Focusing your attention outside your own industry isn't the only way to encourage creative thinking. Many people find inspiration in art, in music, nature, even yoga. It doesn't matter where you find it, what's important is that you do find it and foster it. Sure, it's easier to stick to what you know but in the long run, that just makes you a dull person which in turn translates into your company and ideas becoming dull.

Great leaders are those who encourage their teams to "think out of the box". They create a culture and work environment where it's not only safe to share ideas, but where creative thinking and innovation is rewarded. Appreciate the diversity in generations and employees that your organization represents. Each person may express creativity differently – *Welcome it!* Great leaders know that culture starts at the top, so they walk the Talk. Go ahead, listen to some music, visit an art gallery, shake yourself out of your routine and show your team that you're committed to creative thinking.

CHAPTER TEN

TENACITY -
ARE YOURS BRASS ENOUGH?

"Until one is committed, there is hesitancy, the chance to draw back, always ineffectiveness. Concerning all acts of initiative (and creation), there is one elementary truth that ignorance of which kills countless ideas and splendid plans: that the moment one definitely commits oneself, then providence moves too. All sorts of things occur to help one that would never otherwise have occurred. A whole stream of events issues from the decision, raising in one's favor all manner of unforeseen incidents and meetings and material assistance, which no man could have dreamed would have come his way. Whatever you can do, or dream you can do, begin it. Boldness has genius, power, and magic in it. Begin it now."

William Hutchinson Murray

It's easy to start strong but when challenges arise, how often do you lose momentum? To face the future successfully, great leaders are the ones with the firmest resolve, and the most tenacity. They are the ones who show themselves as flexible and able to adapt rapidly to changes in direction and approach. When you believe something deep down in your bones, tenacity comes easy even in the face of failure, but it's a quality that must be cultivated.

When my father, Paul Witz, passed away I knew I had big shoes to fill. It wasn't until I stepped into the office and was suddenly faced with running what had been his company, that I realized how much he had taught me about tenacity.

I had a choice to make; either step up and continue his legacy or give in to my own self doubt and close the business. Staff and clients looked to me expectantly, in their eyes I could see they were asking the same questions I was. Can he do this? Does he have what it takes? Should we be looking for new careers?

Bills needed to be paid and feelings of insecurity, even panic, needed to be addressed. There was no time to succumb to the dark, even for a moment. I knew that I wanted to protect the legacy my father had left me, but more than that, I realized more clearly, that I sincerely believed in what our company was doing. Being CEO isn't a job to me, it's my life's mission and one that I embrace profoundly. I know you'll understand that because that's one of the reasons you picked up this book. To be the best leader you can be you are going to need to work out your tenacity muscles.

Deeper than optimism and confidence, tenacity fuels persistence, the ability to keep pushing forward until your idea or initiative reaches what Malcolm Gladwell (2002) calls *The Tipping Point*. According to Gladwell, the tipping point "is that magic moment when an idea, trend or social behavior crosses a threshold, tips and spreads like wildfire." Tenacity is hanging on when others doubt you, giving that extra effort at a critical moment, pushing yourself beyond what you thought you were capable of accomplishing.

Let's assume that you're reading this book and having some 'aha moments'. Maybe you're recognizing areas where your preferred leadership style isn't working, where compassion might be the key to unlocking an employee's potential or where a solid dose of humility could repair a relationship. You think anything less than a 100% commitment to doing things differently isn't going to take some tenacity on your part? When you stumble through a conversation trying out a different leadership style only to be met with less than stellar results, it will take every effort not to digress. When you publish your latest piece of thought leadership for the world to see and you find out the competition made a few changes and is taking credit for it, you may immediately revert to hording ideas. It's darkest before the dawn as the saying goes, and it takes the average person 28 days of consistent practice to adopt a new habit. To be successful you're going to need to dig into your well of tenacity and stick it out. Great leaders do. They know when to lean in and they know when to walk away.

Seth Godin in his book *The Dip* (2007) discusses the difference between strategic quitting and quitting, when the going gets rough. Successful companies and leaders are those who, when they find themselves at a plateau, are willing to give up tactics that aren't working without abandoning the end goal. Remember the story of the gold miner who quit just three feet short of one of the richest mines in Colorado? As Hill wrote in his famous book *Think and Grow Rich* (1937), an uncle of R. U. Darby, in the midst of the gold rush, found a large vein in the mountainside and put together the team and machinery request to mine it. At first they were very successful but suddenly, the vein of gold disappeared and no matter the amount of desperate drilling, they were unable to relocate it. They gave up and sold the machinery to a "junk man" for a few hundred dollars and went home. As Hill tells the story, the junk man decided to call in a mining engineer to look at the mine and do some calculations. The engineer was able to show the man that the project had failed, not because the vein was dry, but because the Darbys weren't familiar with fault lines. By shifting the drilling by three feet and beginning again, the junk man netted millions in dollars because the Darbys gave up without getting expert counsel.

Think about that story the next time you want to give up, but unless you can be the best in the world like Godin (2007) suggests, it's time to consider the options.

CHAPTER ELEVEN

TRANSPARENCY -
IT'S NOT ABOUT MONEY

In the 90s the term 'open book management' gained traction and leaders were encouraged not only to share their financial reports with employees, but to adopt the belief that "companies perform better when its people see themselves as partners in the business rather than as hired hands" (Case, 1998). But today's world is demanding more. More than just information and encouraging employees to think and act like owners. Today's world, and tomorrow's generations want transparency. And if they don't get it from you, trust me, they will find it somewhere else.

When I took over my father's company, I knew that in order to keep the doors open and retain our clients and staff, I was going to have to come face to face with the truth. The company was in debt and long time staff members were extremely insecure in the future of the organization. It wasn't that they didn't believe in the vision but rather, would they buy into me as their new leader? Were they prepared to put their own futures at risk by giving me the chance? No longer was I the boss's son, the outspoken master trainer and friend to all. I was responsible for the financial future of the organization and the families of my team. There was much at stake. I took a deep breath, gathered the entire company together and told them the truth. I told them what the financial situation was and I shared my vision for taking the company out of the red and into the black. I told them I had fears but that I had faith that if we came together as a team we would be successful. I asked them to stand with me. To recognize that I was human, that I was bound to make mistakes. I told them that their trust in me would not be taken lightly. I told them of the risks we would all be taking and that I understood if the risk seemed too high for some. I listened with compassion as my staff shared their fears as well as ideas. Most of all, I made a commitment at that moment, that I would always be transparent.

Being transparent is a powerful leadership quality that helps build deeper and more trusting relationships. When people can see the real you, beyond your title or job description, it changes things. If you're really committed to becoming a great leader and cultivating the qualities of compassion, humility and servant leadership that we've been talking about, transparency will add a dimension of trust between you and those you lead that would otherwise be non-existent or worse, false.

The reason many leaders, especially Boomer leaders, are uncomfortable with transparency is because "they believe they will be viewed as less authoritative; that the credentials they worked so hard to attain will lose their power and leverage" (Llopis, 2012). This narrow thinking is dangerous especially to those with Generation Y and Z employees. These younger more outspoken generations demand openness, honesty and the truth, if they are going to put their energy and commitment into a company. More than that, they need to buy into the leader as a person and not just "the boss". It's clear from all the research available that money isn't the motivational tool it was once thought of. What makes team members and clients loyal is their relationship with you, and you'll never achieve that if you don't open up and let them in.

Share your successes, your failures, your strengths and your weaknesses. Show them that you've been where they are and that you understand what they need not only at work, but as people. I guarantee you'll start attracting more like-minded team members, solve problems faster, have more fulfilling relationships and see higher levels of performance across the board. Don't be afraid to tell your team the truth about your business. Energize them. Adapt your communication style to your audience.

Every week I meet with my entire team and go over the books. They share in the successes and feel just as accountable for the losses as I do. They have ownership and feel driven to succeed as much for themselves as for the entire team. They know what a good month means and they know what a bad month means. We laugh and strategize and solve problems together. We depend on each other. There is nothing they can't ask me and they are confident that I share all the information I have that would affect their work.

It's easy to say that people should leave their personal issues at home but it's completely unrealistic to suggest that it's a successful strategy. While I'm not advocating so much personal sharing that performance suffers, I'm encouraging you as the great leader you aspire to be, to promote a culture of openness, compassion and authenticity. It won't always net you the results you want but it will solidify your position as a leader of multiple generations that the future demands.

A short caveat: As a by-product of transparency, you will find that you may lose certain staff or other relationships. Sometimes people simply can't handle the stress of thinking and feeling like an owner. They aren't prepared to be kept up at night when things aren't going smoothly or they don't feel they can take the risk with you. That's okay, encourage it. When my company was in the thick of its rebirth, we graciously said goodbye to a few employees who just couldn't stomach the ups and downs. They found more appropriate positions that offered more stability and we found that it bonded those who stayed to fight more closely.

CHAPTER TWELVE

RISK TAKING -
WITH OR WITHOUT
A PARACHUTE

"Only those who risk going too far can possibly find out how far they can go."

– T.S. Eliot

When was the last time you took a risk? A real risk? Something that made your heart pound and your palms sweat? Maybe it was a business opportunity that could have a huge payoff if it was successful or disastrous if it failed. Maybe it was risking your own ego and embracing transparent leadership like the last chapter suggests. Letting your team see the real you, warts and all. I hope so, and I hope you'll acquire a taste for taking risks in all aspects of your life.

Sure, ideas and approaches can fail. Indeed they do. But nothing great has ever been accomplished without some element of risk. Leaders in the future will thrive not by taking fewer risks but by making sure the risks they take are calculated and managed. No more dismissing ideas and innovations by "what if" and "doomsday scenarios." Boomers, take note, you may learn a lot about risk taking from your younger counterparts. They are growing up in a world where unpredictability and upheaval are the norm. They've seen companies taken down by personal scandal and social causes garner world-wide attention from a post on Instagram. They aren't likely to back away from a risk but instead will charge forward with their youthful optimism, their spontaneous selves, swinging for the fence. As their leader, embrace it!

One of the areas where we at Witz Education are seeing the impact of risk-taking is in the arena of sales. Old school dog and pony shows and "all about us" marketing brochures, aren't getting the job done any more. Customers want solutions and ideas before they open their wallets. We are no longer in the information age where he who has the most information is king. With the Internet providing us with information through a couple of mouse clicks and content being freely streamed from sources around the globe, companies that openly share information instead of hoarding it, will be the ones who thrive. Leaders of the future must take the plunge and risk giving their knowledge away first, in order to engage with prospects. Sales scenarios will become less about trying to pin down a customer's "budget threshold" and more about genuine collaborative problem solving. It shouldn't surprise you that in a recent survey we conducted, we found that 86% of executives researched a company online before even agreeing to meet and even more executives said that they give credence to those companies who openly share their knowledge, without asking for something in return.

What does this mean for leaders? It means that you have to take the risk that the information and knowledge you share may very well end up in your competitor's hands, or that prospective customers will simply decide to "do it" themselves. Boomer and even Gen X sales people struggle with this. At what point does the reward mitigate the risk? The following story should shed some light.

A client of ours had recently hired a new sales person for their consulting department. A woman who has over 20 years of experience selling large scale projects to companies, but whose approach was fundamentally different than how her Gen Y boss conducted business development. As part of her training, the CEO brought her along on the next available opportunity. The company they had made contact with was a big opportunity for them and as the door opener they offered to host a brainstorming session on a topic that was concerning their prospect's business. The complimentary half day session was met with great response and my client's company was invited to continue the conversation.

A meeting was set up with the CEO and VP of Finance from the prospect's company, the CEO and new sales rep from my client's company and myself. I had been brought in to help bridge some communication hurdles my client was having with the sales team. During the conversation, it became noticeably uncomfortable as the discussion kept being interrupted by the new sales person trying to "nail down a budget" and "close the sale". We had to reel her in, before the opportunity to become a strategic partner with this new company was lost. Instead of presenting the prospect with a corporate overview of what we could do for them as traditional sales people do, my client was more interested in learning about what their goals were and what they thought their challenges would be. Ideas and suggestions were flying around the room. It was great. But in the sales rep's mind, they were taking too big of a risk by being open with ideas and information, without being paid and it made her extremely uncomfortable. Finally, the client turned to her and said, "Listen, if we didn't find value in what you guys have shared with us, we wouldn't even be having this conversation. We aren't interested in buying an off the shelf package of services from some random consultant. We want to work with a company who understands us and what we want to accomplish. We want a company that is committed to designing solutions that will help us achieve our goals. Because you have been and are so willing to share information and ideas, we think that company is you." Whew!

Back at the office, I sat down with the saleswoman and the CEO and we talked about what had happened. It was a huge moment. She was beginning to see how the payoff was bigger and the commitment was deeper, all because we were willing to take a risk and provide them with solutions before any contract was signed. The task for the CEO would be to use a Nurturing Parent and Adult leadership style as opposed to his default Spontaneous Child state, to encourage her to try this new approach and provide support when it seemed unnatural, as it would feel until it became a habit. The saleswoman was expecting feedback from a Critical Parent and was noticeably impressed when she received guidance instead of criticism.

I'm not suggesting you jump into a new approach without knowing what you want to accomplish. Great leaders know how to consider opportunities and risks through a wider perspective and manage them. If you as the leader are willing to take a risk and foster a culture where risks are thoroughly assessed, where it's safe to share unconventional ideas and failures are embraced as learning opportunities, you'll be better prepared to face the future. Sure, it's risky and you may fall flat on your face but think about what you'll gain.

CHAPTER THIRTEEN

WORLD PERSPECTIVE

I've been extremely fortunate in my life to have had the opportunity to travel. By travel I don't mean staying at a resort in the Caribbean (although I highly recommend that too!) but rather travelling and working in countries where I was immersed in the culture. Learning from cultures and communities vastly different from my own has given me a much wider lens from which to view the world and it's a quality great leaders embody. Look around you. I'm guessing that you not only have multiple generations in your workplace but that your team is diverse; coming from a range of cultural backgrounds. Don't think for a moment that this diversity doesn't impact your ability to lead and your ability to adapt your communication style quickly and efficiently. Some cultures have preferred leadership styles that are ingrained from birth.

Adopting a world perspective is akin to recognizing the difference between someone being book-smart or street-smart. Both have value but genius happens when the two perspectives can work together collaboratively. Being a great leader today and in the future requires that you get out from behind your desk and open your eyes to the world. Maybe you don't care for the news or don't particularly like flying, that's fine. A world perspective can be gained in many different ways and all it requires is openness and curiosity.

I have a client who grew up in South Africa and was accustomed to sleeping with a rifle under his pillow. Not only does he view the world differently than I, those experiences influence his leadership style significantly. He's highly competitive and isn't the type to back down from a challenge which has served him well. He can also be quite confrontational and his default Angry Child leadership style is often met with strong push back. He says things like "I can't stand that you see things from such a narrow view." Working with him on how to adapt his approach in the context of the players and situations has not only been fun, it has served to broaden my own understanding of human behavior. It also reinforces my belief that it is the responsibility of the leader to adapt, not to expect others to adapt to you.

As you can tell, this book at its core is more about relationships and communication and less about generations. Being able to get to know your team, where they come from, and where they want to go, so that you can help them get there. That's leadership. And great leaders recognize that if they aren't open to exploring the world through the eyes of a variety of people, generations and perspectives, their futures will be limited. Twenty years ago, unless you were glued to the international news, you weren't likely to know about a plane crash in Turkey or an earthquake in the Philippines. We didn't care what haircut celebrities were sporting nor were we likely to consider a woman for CEO. The world was different and it wasn't nearly as accessible as it is today. Great leaders take advantage of this!

Today, project teams can consist of people in different countries around the world. Huge companies are run out of people's spare rooms with their administrative assistant located in Germany or India. The most innovative leaders will encourage this wider more global perspective in themselves and in those they lead. Generations Y and Z are already adept at this and if encouraged and allowed, will add a depth and richness to your organization's culture. Embrace their diversity, learn about their backgrounds, and listen to their ideas. Watch more news and if you don't like flying, then book a train tour across the country. It never ceases to amaze me the number of people who have never been out of their current city. Just because you watch The Amazing Race on TV doesn't mean you're experiencing the world.

The challenge for leaders is to know their own backgrounds and learn how to relate to the differences in culture and style, without sacrificing their objectives. Nuances in behavior and language can have a huge impact on communication and must be taken seriously. Think about Americans and Canadians. We share more things in common than not but when I run training and coaching programs for my American clientele, my delivery approach is extremely different. Tactics that the average Canadian might find overtly assertive, my American colleagues wouldn't bat an eyelash at. That isn't to say that one style is better than the other, it isn't. They are just different. Businesses run differently in Toronto than they do in Calgary or Vancouver. The same goes for New York versus Chicago or Kansas City. Great leaders are able to see and appreciate the unique nuances that show up. Whether you're doing business in one country or around the world, great leaders recognize that cultural values impact every aspect of relationship building. If you can't relate, you lose out.

CHAPTER FOURTEEN

COMMUNICATION TIPS FOR THE GENERATIONS

"The single biggest problem in communication is the illusion that it has taken place" - George Bernard Shaw

In every course I teach or talk I give, I always ask the room what the two key components are for effective communication. I get answers like respect, calm, listening, speaking kindly. It is all of those things and none of those things. The two principles of effective communication are and always will be understanding and comfort.

If I am yelling at you and throwing a chair across the room but you understand me and are comfortable with that, then we are communicating effectively. If you are rambling on and on and I am sitting silently shaking my head up and down not saying a word in return but I am comfortable and understanding you, we are communicating effectively. Effective communication is never about what you are intending but about how you are being received.

As leaders, the key to keeping a diverse workplace population interested, motivated and committed is communication. Psychologist Dr. Paula Butterfield of Columbus, Ohio says that working across generations is hard for many managers. "It can challenge beliefs and values they've always accepted, and squeeze them between the twin rocks of change and conflict." The tools they use, especially communication, can make or break their level of success. "Leaders who understand the conditions that shaped each

85

generation and the value and beliefs that flowed from those conditions will have a handy set of tools in creating strong relationships and teams for getting things done."

How Leaders Can Communicate with Traditionalists (the Silent Generation)

It can be uncomfortable for you to manage others who are your seniors. It can feel like telling your parents what to do. We must work on mutual respect, trust and sharing, because Traditionalists are private by nature. Remember, they believe in putting in their time and working hard. To successfully lead a Traditionalist, we must seek the hard-won wisdom and advice of our elder peers.

Communication Tips:

- Build trust through inclusive language (we, us)

- As a leader, your word is your bond, so focus on being true to your word

- Use face-to-face communication as much as possible

- Try using more formal, concrete language

- Don't waste their time; they have a job to do. Get straight to the point

- Allow time for them to share their innermost thoughts and ideas

How Leaders Can Communicate with Baby Boomers:

Author Howard Smead says that Boomers are "the most egocentric generation in the history of mankind." Because of their volume (76.8 million born between 1946 and 1964), Baby Boomers have reshaped the workplace environment. Sharing information with Boomers can be difficult at times because egos may get in the way. Remember, their work is their life and they are committed to climbing the ladder of success.

Communication Tips:

- Boomers are the "show me" generation, so use body language to communicate

- Speak in an open, direct style

- Answer questions thoroughly and expect to be pressed for details

- Avoid controlling, manipulative language

- Present options to show flexibility in your thinking

- They expect respect: be patient, polite, and gracious

- Communicate via phone, email or in-person

- Be solution oriented

- Present the facts

• Demonstrate integrity & common sense

• Be complimentary and genuine

• Demonstrate accountability in resolving their issues

How Leaders Can Communicate with Generation X:

Gen Xers, born between 1965 and 1980, have looked to their leaders for training, support and guidance. Gen Xers abhor office politics and policies in general. They are independent, entrepreneurial thinkers, ready to move on in a heartbeat. Unlike Boomers, Gen Xers are more interested in quality of life than work, so they will use technology to short-cut their way to success, produce more work in less time and strive for a more balanced life. The marketplace will see a huge shift, as Boomers begin retiring, leaving a large void for Gens X and Y to fill.

Corporate .headhunter Lee Ann Howard, with TMP Worldwide, Executive Search Division, whose flagship brand is Monster.com, says that leaders must create excitement for Gen Xers to step into leadership roles. "Gen Xers are multi-taskers. They are used to a lot of stimuli," Howard says. She adds that leaders must provide three things to keep them motivated – a challenging environment, individual growth and development and assignments that stimulate them."

Communication Tips:

- Learn their language and speak it

- Use email as your primary communication tool

- Ask them for feedback

- Share information with them immediately and often

- Use an informational communication style

- Listen to them – you might learn something

- Be authentic and transparent

- Give them the choice of when and how they prefer to communicate

- Be authentic in your communication

- They seek fun and meaningful interactions

- Prefer informal, casual, high-tech communication

How Leaders Can Communicate with Generations Y & Z:

Generation Y, born between 1981 to 1995 and Generation Z, born between 1996 to 2012, numbering over 90 million strong, represent the new college graduates coming into the workplace. Generation "Why" Guru Eric Chester defines this group of people as "youth who continually question the standards and expectations imposed by society".

With this group, take everything about Gen X and turn it up a notch. These youngsters know no limits. They define the workplace environment as they go. They are highly creative, well educated and technologically advanced. They crave challenge. A national education initiative targeting today's Gen Ys, uses billboards as a primary media vehicle with the headline "Challenge Me." If there is a faster way to do it, Gen Y will find it.

Communication Tips:

- Use action verbs to challenge them
- Don't talk down to them
- Show them respect and they will respect you
- Use visual communication to motivate them and keep them focused
- Constantly seek their feedback to make them feel involved
- Use humor, reassure them you don't take yourself too seriously
- Encourage them to explore new paths or options
- Set clear expectations, goals, targets, etc.
- Give ownership of tasks and provide structure
- Diversify tasks & role to offer challenges
- Offer meaningful work & speak to impact
- Develop relationship & positively reinforce performance

For detailed information on each of the five generations at work today visit our website, **www.witzeducation.com**

CHAPTER FIFTEEN

PUTTING IT ALL TOGETHER

"You never change things by fighting the existing reality. To change something, build a new model that makes the existing model obsolete" Buckminster Fuller

Leaders of today and the future have a huge opportunity ahead. By embracing and learning the qualities of exceptional leaders as shared in this book, you'll be equipped to not only survive but thrive. With five generations at work, complete with their unique demands and skill sets, it's even more important for leaders to understand how their communication styles can affect and influence their success.

When you can get really honest with yourself and see yourself through the eyes and hearts of your team, brilliance will be born. Encourage dialogue, engage in uncomfortable conversations, and try out the different ego states. I guarantee you will see more progress than you ever thought possible. Instead of dismissing a person as "an old fashioned Boomer" or a "lazy Gen Y" you will start to see the gifts and strengths that each generation brings to the table. When you're able as the leader to see your team members as individuals, you can create partner teams based on complimentary values and understanding. Imagine the loyalty and trust you'll inspire.

Open your office door, get out into the streets – embrace the future with all its nooks and crannies. Be persistent, making changes and modifying your default communication style takes time and practice. When I started it was easy to fall into a Critical Parent type of leader, that's what I had grown up with and been influenced by. My natural personality is more in-line with Spontaneous Child but I needed to learn how to balance and adapt to my audiences. As I began learning about people and particularly communication and behavior, it became clear that if I wanted to be successful I was going to have to be the one to adapt. As uncomfortable as it was, I started letting team members in behind the scenes at the office. Now, instead of employees I have a dedicated team of partners whose trust and loyalty have helped grow our business ten fold.

Remember our sales executive from Chapter 12? With some time and practice, she began embracing her Spontaneous Child style and taking risks. The results have been amazing. No longer is she afraid of giving away ideas or information, she shares them with everyone! And this approach has made her a sought after resource both internally and with her customer base. Not to mention that she now has the best sales numbers she's ever experienced.

Think back to our manufacturing company in Chapter 9. When they opened their minds and became more curious, their creativity took root. Now they are recognized as one of the most innovative and approachable manufacturers in North America. Change doesn't happen overnight but just as the old maxim says "water always wins against the rock in the long run", it can be done.

[S]aid the boy: `he learnt how quite soft water, by attrition over the years will grind strong rocks away. in other words, that hardness must lose the day.' (Brecht)

Great leaders possess dazzling social intelligence, a desire for change, and above all else, a vision for greatness. No one is running out of the closet declaring themselves a "bad leader", but it is those who can acknowledge their flaws, and have a burning desire to be better, who will succeed above all others.

One day, when all is said and done, and there are people collected around your grave to say their final goodbyes, they will not be there to honour the power you wielded or the numbers you crunched or the products you launched. They will be there to honor the power of your character, the number of lives you touched and the dreams you launched.

ACKNOWLEDGEMENTS

To my best friend and wife Leya whom people call my handbrake in life. If it weren't for the calm and fortitude you brought into my life, I would have never grown up. I would never have had the guts to teach, coach and run a business in the competitive leadership world. You make me better every day and I am so grateful for that.

To my mother who is an amazing lady. You raised me to be the best man I could be and your unwavering support and encouragement helps me in my quest to become the best possible business man, partner, son, brother and friend I can. Mom, I would never be where I am without you, frankly I'd probably still be slinging drinks at Club Med. Thank you.

To my father whose mark on the world remains fierce. I am reminded of you every day by someone's fond memory or heartwarming story. Thank you for guiding me in business and in life. You impacted so many people so profoundly and I am grateful to have been one of them. I miss you but hope you know that I take on the challenge of continuing your legacy with pride and inspiration.

To my team of all stars at Witz Education who amaze me every day with their commitment and dedication. Every great leader has an even better team behind them. Thank you for your hard work, your consistent performance, for sharing in my vision and most of all for supporting and encouraging me as your leader. I could not do this without you.

To man's best friend, Marley, my loving dog who has taught me so much about trust and loyalty. Thank you for always standing proudly at my side, and sometimes dragging me down the sidewalk.

Finally, to my clients and you the reader, the men and women who aspire to be great leaders, thank you for letting me into your lives. May you grow in your own development as leaders of strong qualities and be met with the success you desire.

Made in the USA
Columbia, SC
27 September 2017